Who Pooped? in the Cascades

Written by Gary D. Robson
Illustrated by Robert Rath

FARCOUNTRY
PRESS

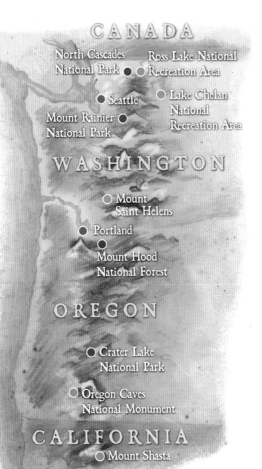

CANADA

North Cascades
National Park
Ross Lake National
Recreation Area
Seattle
Lake Chelan
National
Recreation Area
Mount Rainier
National Park

WASHINGTON

Mount
Saint Helens
Portland
Mount Hood
National Forest

OREGON

Crater Lake
National Park
Oregon Caves
National Monument

CALIFORNIA

Mount Shasta
Lassen Volcanic
National Park

To my wonderful wife, Kathy.
Having you with me makes every
research trip and book signing better!
- Gary

For Lucy and Thomas,
my poop experts.
- Robert

ISBN 10: 1-56037-362-8
ISBN 13: 978-1-56037-362-9

© 2013 by Farcountry Press
Text © 2013 by Gary D. Robson
Illustrations © 2013 by Farcountry Press

For more information on our books,
write Farcountry Press, P.O. Box 5630, Helena, MT 59604;
call (800) 821-3874; or visit www.farcountrypress.com.

Book design by Robert Rath.
Created, produced, and designed in the United States.
Manufactured by Everbest Printing, 334 Huanshi Road South,
Dachong Western Industrial District, Panyu, Guangdong, China
June 2013
Printed in China.

"**A**re we there yet?" Michael squirmed in the back seat. "I really have to go to the bathroom!"

"Hang on," said Dad. "We're almost there—and we have a big surprise for you!"

"A surprise?" Michael asked.

Mom said, "Yes, May's family is taking a trip in the Cascades, too, and we're meeting them at the campground."

"My best friend is here and you didn't tell me?" Michael groused.

the STRAIGHT POOP

The Cascade Mountains stretch over 700 miles from northern California to British Columbia. They include some of the highest peaks in the U.S., like 14,410-foot Mount Rainier.

"We started at the south end of the Cascades, at Lassen Peak. May and her parents started at North Cascades National Park in Washington. We're meeting here at Mount Hood in Oregon."

"Can we go hiking when we get there?" Michael asked.

"That's enough, Emily," said Mom. "Nobody's getting eaten by anything."

Michael was excited about hiking around Mount Hood, but Emily was right. He was a little scared.

"In my wildlife book, the mountain lions do look kind of scary," he admitted.

"Aren't you afraid of being eaten by a big scary mountain lion?" teased Michael's big sister Emily.

Finally, after the long drive,
they arrived at the campground.

"There's May," Emily said.
"Now Michael can bug her
instead of me."

Michael and May compared what animals they'd
seen so far on their trips. May's parents said it was
okay for her to hike with Michael and Emily's family.

"We have seen a lot of animals on our trip, May, but we've seen even more of their sign. Have you?" Dad asked.

BLACK-TAILED DEER

ERMINE

May was puzzled. "Sign? Like a sign at the zoo?" she asked.

"Dad's talking about clues that animals leave behind," Michael explained. "They're called 'sign.'"

GREAT
HORNED
OWL

"Here's a good example of animal sign," explained Mom. "Do you know what made this nest?"

"That doesn't look like any bird nest I've ever seen," said Emily.

"Maybe this will give you a clue," said Dad.

"That's bunny poop, just like I always have to clean from Velvet's cage at home," said Michael.

"Right," smiled Mom. "This is a mountain cottontail rabbit nest."

the STRAIGHT POOP

Rabbits eat their own scat! They do this to get as much nutrition from the food as they can. The little brown balls are scat that's already been through the rabbit twice.

"This poop over here must be from a really big rabbit," said May.

"Actually," explained Dad, "that's deer scat."

"*Scat?* What's scat?" asked May.

"Scat is what scientists call poop," Mom told her. "Rabbits make little round balls, and deer make bigger scat that looks more like brown jellybeans."

BLACK-TAILED DEER

MOUNTAIN COTTONTAIL RABBIT

DEER SCAT

COTTONTAIL SCAT

JELLYBEANS

"Even though deer are a lot bigger than rabbits, their scat is only about twice as big," Dad explained. "If you are really quiet and look at the meadow behind me, you might see the black-tailed deer that left this scat."

the STRAIGHT POOP

Black-tailed deer are a type of mule deer. Mule deer get their name from their big ears.

the STRAIGHT POOP

Bat poop is called "guano," and people use it as fertilizer to make their gardens healthy.

"It's starting to get dark," Mom said. "We should head back."

"Will there be bats like we saw at Oregon Caves when it got dark?" Michael asked excitedly.

"There aren't as many Townsend's big-eared bats as we saw by the caves," Dad answered, "but other bats live here, too—little and big brown bats, and silver-haired bats."

As they walked back
toward their tents,
a loud *HOOT* made
the kids jump.

"What was *that*?" said Michael.

"An owl," whispered Dad,
"Right over there."

the STRAIGHT
POOP

Coastal great horned owls can
have wingspans over four feet!

"Wow," said Emily as the owl flew from the tree, "what a huge bird!"

"That's a great horned owl," replied Mom, "One of the biggest owls in the world."

"I think I found owl scat!" Michael called out.

The STRAIGHT POOP

Scientists take apart cough pellets to look at the bones and fur to find out what birds of prey eat.

"It's from the owl, but it isn't scat," said Emily, trying to sound like a scientist. "It's called a cough pellet. Owls swallow little animals whole, and then spit up the bones, fur, and feathers."

"Very good, Emily! These streaks on the tree are the real owl poop," Dad added.

"Owls are not the only birds that make cough pellets," Mom added. "Eagles make them too."

"We saw a bald eagle at Ross Lake," May said. "He was very beautiful. We saw him catch a fish."

The next morning, May's parents went for a walk while May got in the car with Michael and Emily's family.

"We're going to visit a volcano called Mount St. Helens today," Mom told the kids.

"A *volcano*?" Michael asked. "Isn't that d-dangerous?"

"Don't worry. We've already seen volcanoes on this trip," Dad said. Remember our first stop at Lassen Volcanic National Park? Lassen Peak is a volcano, and so is Mount Shasta, which we visited the next day."

"We saw a volcano, too," May added. "My daddy said Mount Rainier is one of the tallest mountains in North America, and it's a huge volcano."

the STRAIGHT POOP

Every volcanic eruption in the "lower 48" United States in recent history was in the Cascades.

"There's Mount St. Helens," said Mom when they arrived. They hiked up a trail to a good view of the volcano.

"Look at that, kids," Dad told them. "When I was a kid, the whole top of that mountain blew off and knocked down trees for miles around. Now everything is growing back and there are new habitats for the plants and animals!"

the STRAIGHT POOP

Mount St. Helens was 1,300 feet taller before it erupted on May 18, 1980.

"Wow," said Emily. But Michael was distracted by animal footprints nearby.

"Look at these tiny footprints" he said.

Emily and May ran over to Michael.

"Those footprints *are* tiny," May said. "They must be from some kind of rodent, like a mouse or squirrel."

"Rodents eat plants and nuts," Mom said. "Take a look at this scat here and tell me if it looks like it's from a rodent."

"It has fur in it like the owl pellet," Michael said.

"True!" smiled Mom. "It's from an animal that hunts other animals—a predator. It's barely bigger than a hotdog, but it is quite a mighty hunter."

"But what kind of predator is that small?"

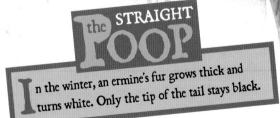

"It's called an ermine," Mom said. "Ermine are a type of weasel. They mostly eat small rodents, but they can even catch and kill rabbits bigger than themselves."

"Ermine look like small otters," Dad added.

"We saw river otters when we went fishing at Lake Chelan!" May piped in excitedly.

"Where's that?" Michael asked.

"In the northern Cascades, up near Canada." Mom said.
"It's the biggest natural lake in Washington, over 50 miles long."

the STRAIGHT POOP

At over 1,400 feet deep, Lake Chelan is also the deepest lake in Washington.

"What do you mean by 'natural' lake, Mom?" Emily asked.

"Some lakes are made by people, and some are made by nature. People make big lakes called 'reservoirs' by building dams across rivers."

Crater Lake is 1,949 feet deep— even deeper than Lake Chelan. It's the deepest lake in the United States!

"Nature has different ways of making lakes, too. Remember where we went fishing a few days ago?" Dad asked.

Emily thought hard for a moment. "Crater Lake? The one you said was made when a volcano blew up?"

"Right! The crater gradually filled with rain and melting snow."

"That's where we saw the funny little animal that looked like a rodent, but you said it was some kind of rabbit," Michael said.

"You mean the pika?" said Dad. "It's not a rabbit, but it's related to them."

the STRAIGHT POOP

Rabbits, hares, and pikas are all part of a big group of animals called lagomorphs.

"I don't think it was a pika that the ermine was chasing, though," Dad said. "Look here!"

"Are those mouse tracks?" May asked. "Or maybe squirrel tracks?"

"Good, May!" said Mom from behind them. "If you stand up quietly and look here, you can see what kind of animal made the tracks."

Michael jumped to his feet and a flying squirrel launched from the tree trunk.

"You scared him!" said Emily.

"What is that?" asked May.

"It's a flying squirrel," said Mom. "They can't really fly, but they can stretch out the skin between their front and back legs and glide on the wind like a paper airplane."

Michael ran a few steps behind the squirrel and saw much bigger tracks. He stopped and asked, "Are these dog tracks?"

"They are from a type of dog," Dad explained. "You can tell because there are four toes with a pad on both the front and back feet, and you can see claw marks.

"If you look at the scat over here it tells the rest of the story," Mom added.

"This scat looks like dog poop," May said, "but it's got a bunch of funny stuff in it."

"That's hair and bones from the animals they've been eating," Mom explained.

"The tracks are too big to be a fox, so they must be from a coyote," Dad finished.

the STRAIGHT
POOP

Coyotes eat just about anything they can catch. They steal leftovers from other predators, too.

Michael called out from down the trail, "I think I found another coyote track."

"That's not a coyote track," said May, catching up. "There are no claw marks. It looks like the bobcat track I saw at North Cascades."

"That's too big to be a bobcat track," said Mom. "I'm pretty sure that's from a mountain lion."

the STRAIGHT POOP

There is one member of the dog family that usually doesn't show claw marks in its tracks: the gray fox. Their small claws are so sharp they can climb trees like a cat.

"Yep," confirmed Dad. "This scrape confirms it."

"What?" Michael gasped. "Is the mountain lion around here somewhere? Maybe we should go back to the car...."

"Don't worry," said Mom. "Even if the mountain lion is still nearby, it wouldn't bother a big group of people like us."

the STRAIGHT POOP

Mountain lions have different names in different parts of the country. They're also called panthers, painters, cougars, pumas, and catamounts.

"Mountain lions aren't very common," said Mom. "We're really lucky to see this sign."

"And this is different from most sign," Dad added. "Animals usually leave sign by accident, but this was left on purpose."

"On purpose?" asked Emily.

"It wanted other mountain lions to know whose territory this is, so it scraped the stuff into a pile and peed on it," Dad explained.

The kids looked at each other and all said, "Ewwwwww!"

"Here's another mountain lion sign," said Mom.

"Wow!" said Emily, "That tree is torn up just like my kitty Snowball's scratching post."

"That's right! Mountain lions sharpen their claws just like housecats do," Mom explained.

May spotted something a bit down the trail from the scrape. "Is this mountain lion scat?"

"It sure is," answered Dad. "Good eyes, kiddo! The ground is too hard here to bury the scat."

Michael looked closer. "It has hairs and bits of bone in it, just like the coyote scat," Michael pointed out. "That means they eat other animals."

the STRAIGHT POOP

Mountain lions may be the biggest cat in America, but they still bury their scat just like a housecat.

Emily laid her hand next to the track.
"This mountain lion must be big," she said.

"That's right," Mom said. "A mountain lion weighs as much as I do, and a big one can weigh more than Dad!"

As they ate dinner that night, everyone talked about how much fun they had.

"We didn't see very many animals," said Emily, "but it seemed like we did!"

Everyone laughed when Michael said, "And I didn't get scared once!"

45

TRACKS and

COYOTE

FRONT

BACK

NO DENT

Coyote tracks look like dog tracks. They have four toes on each foot. Their claw marks usually show above each toe.

Scat is very dark in color and usually contains bits of hair. Scat is tapered on the ends.

MOUNTAIN LION

LEADING TOE

DENT

FRONT

BACK

Tracks are bigger than a coyote's. They have four toes on each foot. Claws do not make marks in their tracks.

Scat usually either buried or surrounded with scratch marks from where the mountain lion tried to bury the scat.

ERMINE

FRONT

BACK

Tiny tracks are about the size of a dime and show five toes per foot.

Scat is black and ropey, often bent and twisted.

BALD EAGLE

Tracks feature three slender toes pointing forward and one toe pointing backward. Claw indentations do not touch the toe prints.

Scat is runny and white.

Cough pellets are up to a half-inch long and contain hair.

GREAT HORNED OWL

Tracks show four toes: two pointing forward and two back or sideways.

Scat is runny and white.

Cough pellets contain fur and bones.

ANIMALS THAT EAT OTHER ANIMALS

SCAT NOTES

TOWNSEND'S BIG-EARED BAT

No tracks.

Scat is thin, twisted light brown/golden pellets. Sometimes shimmery. Often has insect parts scattered around it.

MOUNTAIN COTTONTAIL RABBIT

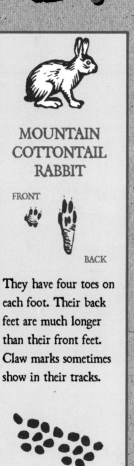

FRONT

BACK

They have four toes on each foot. Their back feet are much longer than their front feet. Claw marks sometimes show in their tracks.

Scat is a pile of small brown balls.

PIKA

FRONT

BACK

Tracks are like small rabbit tracks. Different from rodent tracks because back foot only has four toes.

Scat is tiny round brown balls, about half the size of rabbit scat.

BLACK-TAILED DEER

Pointy split-hoof tracks.

Scat is oval-shaped, like jellybeans.

NORTHERN FLYING SQUIRREL

FRONT

BACK

Tracks usually only show up in snow.
Four toes on front foot, five on back.
Tracks often start with a "snow angel" where the squirrel landed.

Scat is tiny brown bits about the size of a grain of rice.

ANIMALS THAT EAT INSECTS

ANIMALS THAT EAT PLANTS

ABOUT the AUTHOR and ILLUSTRATOR

GARY ROBSON lives in Montana near Yellowstone National Park, where he and his wife own a bookstore and tea bar. Gary has written dozens of books and hundreds of articles, mostly related to science, nature, and technology.
www.robson.org/gary

ROBERT RATH is a book designer and illustrator living in Bozeman, Montana. Although he has worked with Scholastic Books, Lucasfilm, and The History Channel, his favorite project is keeping up with his family.

Who Pooped in the Park?™

BOOKS IN THE
WHO POOPED IN THE PARK?™
SERIES:

Acadia National Park
Big Bend National Park
Black Hills
Cascades
Colorado Plateau
Death Valley National Park
Glacier National Park
Grand Canyon National Park
Grand Teton National Park
Great Smoky Mountains National Park
Northwoods
Olympic National Park
Red Rock Canyon National Conservation Area
Rocky Mountain National Park
Sequoia and Kings Canyon National Parks
Shenandoah National Park
Sonoran Desert
Yellowstone National Park
Yosemite National Park